X³

Meet the germs

Different germs can make you ill in different ways.

I give you a cold.

Cold

5

How germs invade

Your skin stops most germs from getting inside your body. But ...

 Some germs are in the air. You breathe them in.

Sneezes can spread germs.

2 Some germs can be swallowed.

Germs grow on food that is old or not cooked properly.

There are germs on your hands. You should wash your hands before you eat. This photo of a hand shows in white where the germs are.

3 Some germs can get into open cuts.

Your skin forms a scab over the cut. It stops germs getting in.

What do germs do?

When a germ gets inside you it makes lots more germs.

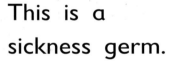

This is a sickness germ.

The germs make **poison**.
This makes you feel ill.

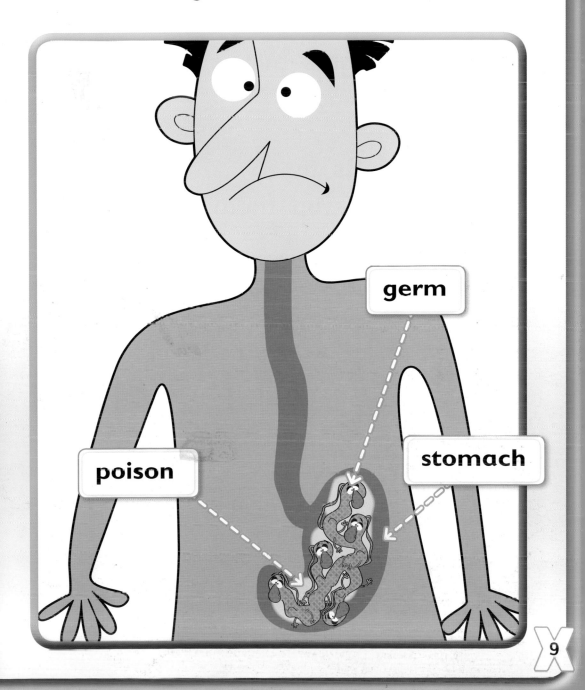

Your body fights back

Your body fights germs in different ways.

1 Some **cells** fit to germs to stop them.

germ

cell

cell

2 Some cells eat germs.

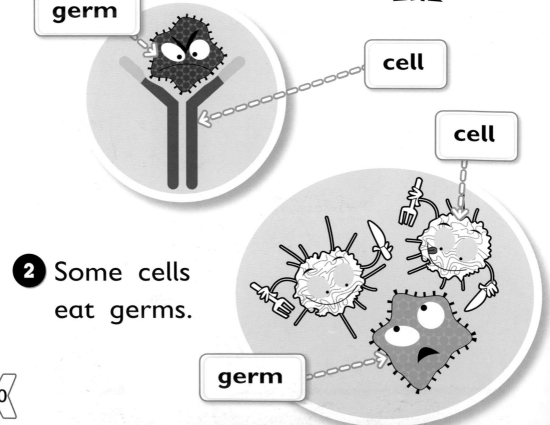

germ

3 Some cells close up any cuts.

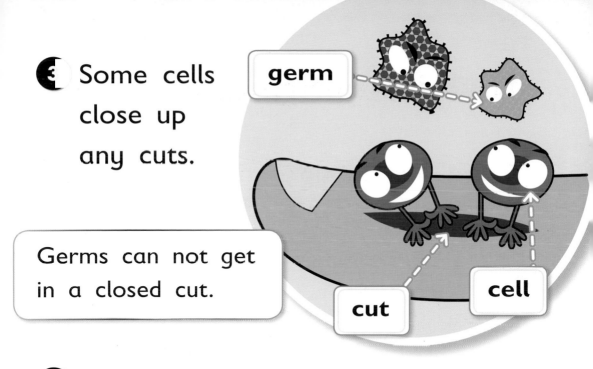

germ

Germs can not get in a closed cut.

cut

cell

4 Your body heats up as it fights the germs.

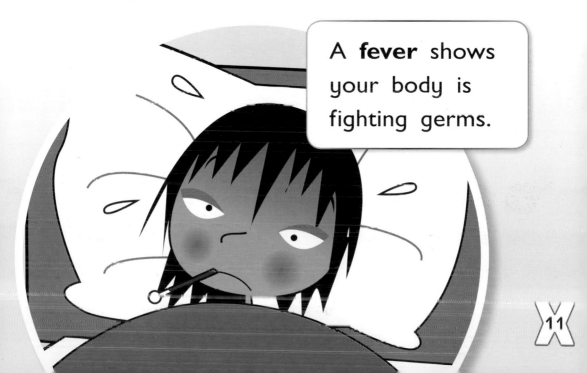

A **fever** shows your body is fighting germs.

Call the doctor

Doctors can help our bodies to fight some germ **invaders**. Your doctor sometimes gives you medicine to kill germs.

Wash to win!

These are the best ways to stop germ invaders.

1 Use a tissue when you cough or sneeze.

2 Wash your hands before you eat.

3 Never eat food that is too old or not properly cooked.

4 Keep cuts clean and wear a plaster.

5 Wash your hands after you visit the toilet.

Glossary

cells the smallest part of everything that is alive

fever when an illness makes you very hot

healthy not ill

invade to attack

invader attacker

poison something that can harm your body or make you ill

Index